Tactical Today, Strategic Tomorrow

A Thinking Journal for Professional Growth

Camelle ilona FRSA

Copyright © 2024 by Camelle ilona

All rights reserved.

No part of this book may be reproduced in any form or by any electronic or mechanical means, including information storage and retrieval systems, without written permission from the author, except for the use of brief quotations in a book review.

"For my friends stepping up from tactical to strategic positions, I'm so proud of you!"

Camelle ilona

Foreword

As I sit down to write this foreword, I am filled with immense pride and joy. I have had the privilege of knowing Camelle for many years. I have watched her grow, evolve, and transform into the remarkable professional she is today. It has been a unique journey, and I am honoured to have played a part in her development as her mentor in business and beyond.

With a career spanning several decades, mainly as a Business Consultant in the fashion industry, I have worked with countless companies, both large corporations, government and enthusiastic startups. One of the most common challenges I've seen is the difficulty many face in the planning stages and pivoting phases of their ventures. Far too often, these promising entrepreneurs lose their way and, regrettably, give up on their dreams.

Foreword

Camelle's book, "Tactical Today, Strategic Tomorrow," is a beacon of hope and guidance for those navigating the tumultuous waters of starting and growing a business and/or making career progress. It offers an insightful and practical approach to transitioning from tactical execution to strategic thinking, which is crucial for long-term success. This publication is not just another business book; it is a valuable contribution to the art of building a successful venture, regardless of the discipline.

What sets this book apart is its accessibility and practicality. Camelle has crafted a collection of journaling prompts and exercises that gently guide readers towards a mindset shift. These tools are designed to fit into the busiest of schedules, making them an indispensable resource for anyone looking to transform their career. From the practicalities of daily life to overarching career aspirations, this book provides a clear framework of prompts to curate your own roadmap to success.

The structured approach Camelle presents is something I wish I had thought of myself. Whether you are at the beginning of your career or looking to make a strategic shift, this book is an invaluable tool. It encourages readers to embrace delegation, adopt a bird's-eye view, and develop the mindset necessary for strategic thinking.

I wholeheartedly believe that "Tactical Today, Strategic Tomorrow" will empower its readers to step confidently into new roles, armed with the skills and mindset needed for

Foreword

success. It is an excellent publication that I am sure will make a significant impact on its readers, just as Camelle has made a significant impact on all who have had the pleasure of knowing and working with her.

David Jones FRSA CText FCFI FCDI FBIM
Essential Business Solutions

Introduction

This book was created out of a conversation with friends who were all stepping into management roles and responsibilities. They were getting stuck straddling the familiar tactical, comfortable, busy work they have been used to and struggling to take the leap into the strategic thinking and decision-making positions they were being offered.

I created this journal to help them think, journal, process and get unstuck. They were being offered these strategic roles because they CAN DO the job but their heads were getting in their own way. My hope was and still is to shift them from being tactical today into being more strategic tomorrow.

Introduction

"I love this concept! Each journaling prompt helped to structure my thoughts which so often spark off in different directions. With this book I get to focus my creative mind on shifting from where I am now, to where I want to be. Instead of being overwhelmed by all the smaller tactical moves I need to make, I get the space to think strategically about making the right moves at the right time and making greater impact."

Andrea Francis, Business Development Manager

How to use this journal

Read the short chapters for context, then journal the prompts, not all will apply.

When journaling think in the context of your work but as you write, flow, depending on what's happening in your life, some questions may apply to another area of your life and that's fine. Sometimes, the root issue is not what is directly in front of us, but rather something else that we need to process.

Be open, enjoy the process and let it stretch you!

Contents

Chapter 1 Tactical and Strategic	15
Chapter 2 Focusing on outcomes	31
Chapter 3 Learning to delegate	45
Chapter 4 Developing a growth mindset	59
Chapter 5 Seeking input from others	73
Chapter 6 Continuous learning	87
Chapter 7 Prioritizing	101
Chapter 8 Being proactive	115
Chapter 9 Fostering a culture of strategic thinking	129
Chapter 10 Measuring progress	143
Bonus Chapter Tomorrow AI is Tactical, so Tomorrow we MUST be Strategic	157
Notes	173
About the Author	175
Booking Camelle ilona	177
Also by Camelle ilona FRSA	179

Chapter 1 Tactical and Strategic

Tactical work is focused on day-to-day activities that directly contribute to achieving short-term goals. Strategic thinking involves looking beyond the immediate tasks and understanding the long-term implications of your actions.

In any professional setting, there are two types of work that individuals engage in - tactical work and strategic thinking.

Tactical work is focused on the day-to-day activities that contribute to achieving short-term goals.

Strategic thinking, on the other hand, involves looking beyond the immediate tasks and understanding the long-term implications of one's actions. Understanding the difference between tactical work and strategic thinking is essential for professionals who want to grow and succeed in their careers.

Tactical work is the foundation of any business. It involves the execution of specific tasks and activities that contribute to overall success. This work is typically routine and requires a high level of attention to detail.

Examples of tactical work include;

- managing daily operations,
- meeting deadlines, and
- completing routine tasks.

Tactical work is essential for an organisation to achieve its immediate goals and objectives.

On the other hand, strategic thinking focuses on an organisation's long-term goals and objectives. It requires individuals to take a broader perspective and think about the big picture.

Strategic thinking involves looking beyond the immediate tasks and understanding the long-term implications of one's actions. It is about **thinking creatively** and **coming up with innovative solutions** for problems.

Examples of strategic thinking include;

- developing long-term business plans,
- identifying new markets, and
- creating innovative products or services.

To understand the difference between tactical work and strategic thinking, it is essential to recognise that there are two distinct types of work that require different skill sets.

Tactical work requires individuals to be:

- detail-oriented,
- efficient, and
- focused on completing specific tasks.

Strategic thinking, on the other hand, requires individuals to be:

- creative,
- innovative, and
- capable of thinking outside the box.

Both types of work are essential for the success of an organisation, and individuals who can balance the two are highly valued.

As an entrepreneur, strategy days were really important for stepping back, reviewing the numbers, having an overview, casting vision and doing quarterly planning. This was the time to plan was tactical work needed to be executed on a daily basis.

One of the key benefits of strategic thinking is that it enables individuals to identify potential problems before they arise. By looking at the big picture, individuals can anticipate challenges and develop proactive solutions to avoid them. This helps organisations to become more resilient and adaptable in the face of change.

> Strategic Thinking encourages innovation and creativity.
>
> @Camelle ilona

By taking a broader perspective, individuals can come up with new ideas and solutions that drive business growth and success. This is essential in today's fast-paced business environment, where innovation is often the key to staying ahead of the competition.

In conclusion, understanding the difference between tactical work and strategic thinking is essential for professionals who want to grow and succeed in their careers. While tactical work is focused on achieving short-term goals, strategic thinking is focused on the long-term success of an organisation. By balancing the two, individuals can drive innovation, anticipate challenges, and achieve long-term success.

10 journaling prompts

1. How do you currently differentiate between tactical and strategic work in your personal and professional life?

2. How do you prioritise your tasks and determine which tasks are more tactical or strategic in nature?

3. For you, what are some of the key characteristics of tactical work? How do these differ from the characteristics of strategic work?

4. What are some of the potential risks or negative consequences of focusing solely on tactical work? How can you personally ensure that you are balancing tactical work with a focus on strategic thinking and long-term planning?

5. How do you ensure that you are not sacrificing long-term success for short-term gains? What strategies do you use to maintain a focus on the bigger picture?

6. How do you communicate the difference between tactical and strategic work to your team members or colleagues? How do you ensure that everyone is aligned and working towards the same goals?

7. What are some of the key skills or competencies that are required for success in tactical work? How do these differ from the skills and competencies required for success in strategic thinking?

8. How do you develop your own skills and competencies in both tactical and strategic work? What resources or tools do you use to improve in these areas?

9. What are some of the potential challenges or obstacles that you may face as you strive to balance tactical work with strategic thinking? How can you overcome these challenges?

10. How do you ensure that you are creating a culture of both tactical excellence and strategic thinking within your personal and professional life? What steps can you take to foster a balance between these two approaches?

Chapter 2 Focusing on outcomes

Strategic thinking is a goal-oriented approach to problem solving. Identify what you want to achieve and work back to identify the steps.

Strategic thinking involves setting clear goals and objectives, developing plans to achieve those goals, and taking proactive steps to execute those plans. By focusing on outcomes, organisations can make better decisions, allocate resources more effectively, and ultimately achieve greater success.

The first step in focusing on outcomes is to identify clear and measurable goals. These goals should be specific, realistic, and achievable. It is important to define the desired outcome in a way that is tangible and measurable, so that progress can be tracked and evaluated over time. Examples of measurable goals might include increasing revenue by a certain percentage, improving customer satisfaction ratings, or reducing production costs by a certain amount.

Once the goals have been established, it is important to work backward to identify the necessary steps to achieve those outcomes. Break the goal into smaller, more manageable tasks and identifying the resources, skills, and expertise that will be needed to complete each task. By breaking down the goal into smaller steps, individuals can create a roadmap to success and work more efficiently towards achieving the desired outcome.

One of the benefits of focusing on outcomes is that it encourages individuals to take a proactive approach to problem-solving. Instead of reacting to problems as they arise, individuals can take a more strategic approach and develop proactive solutions to avoid problems before they occur. By identifying potential roadblocks or obstacles in advance, individuals can develop contingency plans and ensure that progress towards the desired outcome is not derailed.

Focusing on outcomes also enables individuals to be more accountable for their actions and results. By setting clear goals and tracking progress towards those goals, individuals can take ownership of their work and take pride in their accomplishments. This accountability also enables individuals to learn from their mistakes and adjust their approach as needed to achieve the desired outcome.

In conclusion, focusing on outcomes is a critical aspect of strategic thinking. By identifying clear and measurable goals and working backward to determine the necessary steps to achieve those goals, individuals can align their efforts with their objectives and work more efficiently towards success. This approach encourages proactive problem-solving, fosters accountability, and ultimately leads to greater success in both personal and professional endeavours.

> When it comes to your goals:
> BE Brave don't play it safe.
>
> @Camelle ilona

10 journaling prompts

1. What are your current short-term and long-term goals? How do these goals align with your personal and professional aspirations?

2. How do you measure progress towards your goals? What metrics do you use to track success?

3. How do you break down larger goals into smaller, actionable steps? What tools or strategies do you use to ensure that you stay on track?

4. What are some of the potential obstacles or challenges that you may face as you work towards your goals? How can you overcome these challenges?

5. How do you prioritise your tasks and ensure that you are focused on the most important outcomes?

6. How do you adjust your approach if you are not making progress towards your goals? What strategies do you use to stay motivated and persistent?

7. How do you ensure that you are working towards outcomes that are meaningful and aligned with your values and priorities?

8. How do you celebrate and acknowledge your progress towards your goals? What strategies do you use to stay motivated and engaged?

9. What are some of the potential risks or negative consequences of focusing solely on outcomes? How can you ensure that you are balancing outcome-oriented thinking with a focus on process, experience and lessons learnt?

10. How do you ensure that you are not sacrificing your well-being or the well-being of others in pursuit of outcomes? How can you maintain a healthy balance between achievement and self-care?

Chapter 3 Learning to delegate

You can't focus on strategic thinking if you're bogged down with tactical work. Delegate tasks to trusted team members and focus on the bigger picture.

Delegation is a critical skill for anyone who wants to be an effective leader or strategic thinker. In order to achieve success, it is important to recognise that you cannot do everything yourself. By delegating tasks to trusted team members, you can free up your time and mental energy to focus on the bigger picture and more strategic thinking.

Delegation involves identifying tasks that can be completed by others and assigning them to team members who have the skills and resources to complete them successfully. It requires trust in your team and the ability to communicate clearly and effectively to ensure that everyone is on the same page.

One of the key benefits of delegation is that it allows you to prioritise your time and focus on the tasks that require your unique skills and expertise. When you are bogged down with tactical work, - no matter how comfortable and familiar it feels - it will be difficult to find the time and energy to think strategically and make the decisions that will move things forward. By delegating tasks to others, you free up your time and attention to focus on the bigger picture and more strategic thinking.

Another benefit of delegation is that it encourages growth and develops others in your team. By holding on to the tactical tasks you could be hindering someone else growth. When you delegate tasks to others, you are giving them the opportunity to learn, grow and shine in their roles. This can be a powerful motivator for team members, it shows that you trust and value their contributions. It also develops a sense of ownership and pride in their work, which can lead to greater engagement and productivity overall.

However, delegation is not always easy. It requires trust in your team members, clear communication, and the ability to let go of control. It can also be challenging to identify the right tasks to delegate and the right team members to delegate them to. Effective delegation requires a thoughtful approach that takes into account the strengths and weaknesses of your team members, as well as the overall goals and priorities.

To effectively delegate, it is important to communicate clearly and provide team members with the resources and support they need to be successful. This may involve providing training or guidance, setting clear expectations, allowing them to shadow and ask questions, providing ongoing feedback and support. It is also important to recognise and reward the contributions of others, both in terms of individual accomplishments and contributions as a whole.

In conclusion, delegation is a critical skill for anyone who wants to be an effective leader and a strategic thinker. By learning to delegate tasks to trusted team members, you can free up your time and mental energy to focus on the bigger picture and more strategic thinking. Effective delegation requires:

- trust,
- clear communication, and
- a thoughtful approach that considers the strengths and weaknesses of the team.

By mastering the art of delegation, you can become a more effective and successful leader, and help your team achieve greater success.

10 journaling prompts

1. What are some of the tasks that you currently handle that could be delegated to others (list them)? Why have you not yet delegated these tasks? Consider plotting the strengths of the team members around you and against the tasks that need to be delegated.

2. What are some of the benefits of delegation, both for yourself and for your team members?

3. How do you determine which tasks are appropriate to delegate, and which team members are best suited to handle them?

4. What are some of the challenges you have faced in delegating tasks in the past? How have you worked to overcome these challenges? Consider whether you are projecting other people's previous failures when it came to delegation, onto new people in a new situation.

5. How do you communicate your expectations to team members when delegating tasks? What information do you provide to ensure that they are able to complete the task successfully? (Do your best not to make assumptions).

6. How do you monitor progress and provide feedback to team members when they are working on delegated tasks?

7. What are some of the potential risks or negative consequences of delegation? How can you mitigate these risks and ensure that delegated tasks are completed successfully?

8. How can you develop trust and build stronger relationships with team members through delegation? How can you test the delegation waters?

9. What are some of the benefits of empowering team members through delegation? How can this lead to increased engagement and productivity? Can you think a current example?

10. How can you use delegation as a tool for developing the skills and abilities of your team members? How can you provide opportunities for growth and development through delegated tasks?

Chapter 4 Developing a growth mindset

**Embrace new challenges and opportunities.
Be willing to take risks and learn from failure.**

Developing a growth mindset is an essential component of strategic thinking. A growth mindset is all about embracing new challenges and opportunities, being willing to take risks, and learning from failure. It's a mindset that recognises that success is not just about innate ability, but also about hard work, perseverance, and a willingness to adapt and learn.

When you have a growth mindset, you approach challenges and obstacles with a sense of curiosity and a willingness to learn. You don't shy away from new experiences or opportunities simply because they are unfamiliar or outside of your comfort zone. Instead, you embrace them as opportunities to grow and develop.

One of the key benefits of a growth mindset is that it allows you to take risks and learn from failure. When you are willing to take risks, you open yourself up to new opportunities and experiences that can help you grow and develop. And when you inevitably encounter failure along the way, you view it as an opportunity to learn and improve, rather than a setback or a reflection of your abilities.

Another important aspect of a growth mindset is a willingness to seek out feedback and learn from others. When you are open to feedback, you can learn from others' experiences and perspectives, and use that information to improve your own skills and abilities. This can be especially valuable in a team setting, where each team member brings unique perspectives and experiences to the table.

To develop a growth mindset, it's important to be intentional about seeking out new experiences and opportunities, and to approach these experiences with an open mind and a willingness to learn.

One effective strategy for developing a growth mindset is to set learning goals for yourself. This could involve taking on new projects or challenges that require you to learn new skills or acquire new knowledge, keeping your finger in the industry pulse. It could also involve seeking out mentorship or coaching from others who have expertise in areas that you are interested in exploring.

Another effective strategy for developing a growth mindset is to cultivate a sense of curiosity and a desire to learn. This could involve reading books, listening to podcasts, attending seminars, training or workshops, or simply taking the time to explore new ideas and perspectives on your own.

Ultimately, developing a growth mindset is about recognising that success is not just about innate ability, but also about a willingness to learn, adapt, and grow. When you approach challenges and obstacles with this mindset, you open yourself up to new opportunities and experiences that can help you achieve your goals and become the best version of yourself.

10 journaling prompts

1. What does having a growth mindset mean to you?

2. What are some examples of challenges or opportunities that you have embraced in the past?

3. How do you typically react to failure or setbacks?

4. What is one thing you could do today to push yourself outside of your comfort zone?

5. Who is someone you admire for their growth mindset, and why?

6. What are some areas in your life where you feel you have room for growth?

7. How can you reframe your mindset around failure, so that it becomes an opportunity for learning?

8. What is one risk you have been hesitant to take, and what might be holding you back?

9. How can you seek out feedback and learn from others, both personally and professionally?

10. What is one small step you can take today to cultivate a sense of curiosity and desire to learn?

Chapter 5 Seeking input from others

Collaborate with others to gain new perspectives and insights. Seek feedback from those who have experience and expertise in areas that you do not.

As human beings, we have a natural tendency to seek validation and confirmation from others. Seeking input from others is an important part of personal and professional growth. It is a way to gain new perspectives and insights, learn from the experience of others, and develop empathy and understanding.

Collaborating with others can lead to powerful creative solutions to complex problems, as well as an increased sense of accountability and buy-in. When we seek input from others, we are showing that we value their opinions and expertise. This can lead to deeper relationships and a more positive and productive work environment.

One way to seek input from others is to actively collaborate on projects and initiatives. This can involve brainstorming sessions, team meetings, or simply reaching out to others for their feedback and input. By working together, we can achieve better results and develop more effective strategies.

> Showing interest in others tends to make them like you more.
>
> @Camelle ilona

Another way to seek input from others is to actively seek feedback. This can involve asking for feedback from colleagues, mentors, or even customers. By seeking feedback, we can identify areas for improvement and make adjustments to our approach. This can help us to be more effective in our work and achieve better outcomes.

Seeking input from others is also an important way to develop empathy and understanding. By listening to the perspectives and experiences of others, we can broaden our own perspective and gain a deeper understanding of the world around us. This can lead to increased empathy and understanding, as well as better communication and collaboration.

Of course, seeking input from others is not always easy. It can require vulnerability and a willingness to admit that we do not have all the answers. It can also require an openness to new ideas and perspectives, which can challenge our own beliefs and assumptions.

One way to overcome these challenges is to approach seeking input from others with an open and curious mindset. Instead of being closed to one way of doing things, see it as an opportunity to learn and grow. Instead of being defensive or dismissive of new ideas, be open to the possibility that there may be a better way to approach a problem or situation. A fresh perspective leads to innovation.

Another way to overcome these challenges is to be intentional about who we seek input from. We should seek out those who have experience and expertise in areas that we do not, as well as those who have a different perspective or approach to problem-solving. This can help us to gain new insights and ideas that we may not have considered otherwise. Often, when we show that we genuinely value someone's opinion, it opens them up to share more with you and keep you in mind for opportunities they're exposed to.

In conclusion, seeking input from others is an important part of personal and professional growth. By collaborating with others, seeking feedback, and developing empathy and understanding, we can achieve better results and become more effective in our work. It requires vulnerability and a willingness to learn, but the benefits are well worth the effort.

> Private Vulnerability leads to public Authenticity & Authority.
>
> @Camelle ilona

10 journaling prompts

1. Who are the people in your life that you can seek input from?

2. How can you actively collaborate with others to gain new perspectives and insights?

3. What are some areas in your life where you could benefit from seeking feedback from others?

4. How can you overcome the fear or discomfort of seeking input from others?

5. Who are some individuals with experience and expertise in areas that you do not have?

6. How can you show others that you value their opinions and expertise when seeking input from them?

7. What are some examples of times when seeking input from others has led to better outcomes for you?

8. What are some potential drawbacks of not seeking input from others?

9. How can you develop better listening skills when seeking input from others?

10. How can you ensure that you are being intentional about seeking input from a diverse range of perspectives and experiences?

Chapter 6 Continuous learning

Invest in your own development by attending workshops, reading books and articles, and seeking out mentors and coaches.

In today's rapidly evolving world, it is essential to continuously learn and develop new skills to stay competitive in the workforce and in life. Investing in your own development through attending workshops, reading books and articles, and seeking out mentors and coaches can lead to personal and professional growth.

One of the key benefits of continuously learning is the ability to adapt to change. As technology advances and industries evolve, new skills become essential. Continuously learning allows you to stay current and up-to-date with industry trends and best practices. This can lead to increased job security and career advancement opportunities.

Another benefit of continuous learning is personal growth. Learning new skills and knowledge can broaden your perspectives and help you become more well-rounded. It can also boost your confidence and self-esteem, as you become more knowledgeable and skilled in different areas.

Attending workshops is a great way to learn new skills and gain insights from industry experts. Workshops can provide hands-on experience and networking opportunities with like-minded individuals. They can also be a source of inspiration and motivation, as you learn from those who have achieved success in your desired field.

Reading books and articles is another way to continuously learn. There is a wealth of information available on any topic, and reading can help you stay informed and expand your knowledge. *Reading can also stimulate your imagination and creativity, leading to new ideas and solutions to problems.*

Mentors and coaches can provide invaluable guidance and support in your personal and professional development. They can offer insights and advice based on their own experiences, and help you navigate challenges and opportunities. Having a mentor or coach can also provide accountability and motivation, as they help you set and achieve goals.

Continuous learning does not have to be limited to formal education or training. It can also involve taking on new challenges and experiences outside of your comfort zone. This can include volunteering, trying a new hobby, or taking on a leadership role in a community organisation. These experiences can provide opportunities to develop new skills and gain confidence in yourself and your abilities.

To continuously learn, it is important to:

- Make it a priority in your life,
- Set aside time each week to read,
- Attend workshops,
- Meet with a mentor or coach,
- Make a plan for your personal and professional development,
- Set achievable goals for yourself,
- Celebrate your successes and learn from your failures, using them as opportunities for growth and improvement.

In conclusion, continuously learning is essential for personal and professional growth. It allows you to stay current with industry trends, broaden your perspectives, and develop new skills and knowledge. By investing in your own development through attending workshops, reading books and articles, and seeking out mentors and coaches, you can become a lifelong learner and achieve success in all areas of your life.

10 journaling prompts

1. What are some new skills or knowledge areas that you would like to develop?

2. What are some books or articles that you have been wanting to read to learn more about a topic of interest?

3. Who are some people in my network who could potentially be mentors or coaches, and how can you reach out to them (make a list)?

4. What are some upcoming workshops or conferences that you could attend to learn more about a topic you are interested in?

5. What are some online courses or webinars that you could take to develop new skills?

6. What are some hobbies or activities that you have always wanted to try, and how could they help you learn something new?

7. What are some potential barriers that may prevent you from investing in your own development, and how can you overcome them?

8. What are some ways that you can apply what you have learned to you personal or professional life?

9. How can you measure your progress in your learning journey?

10. How can you celebrate your achievements and use you failures as opportunities for growth and improvement?

Chapter 7 Prioritizing

Identify what is most important and focus on those areas. Don't let yourself get distracted by small details that are not critical to achieving your goals.

When it comes to achieving success, prioritisation is key. It's all too easy to get bogged down by the small details that are not critical to achieving our goals. This is why it's important to identify what is most important and focus on those areas.

The first step in prioritisation is to identify your goals. What do you want to achieve? What is most important to you? Once you have identified your goals, it's important to break them down into smaller, more manageable tasks. This will make it easier for you to focus on what is most important and prioritise your time accordingly.

It's also important to understand that not all tasks are created equal. Some tasks are more important than others and require more attention and resources. When prioritising your tasks, it's important to focus on the ones that will have the greatest impact on achieving your goals.

One way to prioritise your tasks is to use the Eisenhower Matrix[1]. This tool helps you to categorise your tasks based on their urgency and importance. The four categories are:

1. Urgent and important: These are the tasks that require immediate attention and should be your top priority.

2. Important but not urgent: These are the tasks that are important but can be scheduled for a later time.

3. Urgent but not important: These are the tasks that are urgent but do not contribute significantly to your goals. Delegate or defer these tasks if possible.

4. Not urgent and not important: These are the tasks that are not critical to achieving your goals. Eliminate or reduce these tasks to free up more time for the important ones.

Another way to prioritise your tasks is to focus on the 80/20 rule. This rule states that 80% of your results come from 20% of your efforts. Identify the 20% of your tasks that contribute the most to achieving your goals and focus your time and resources on those tasks.

Prioritisation also means saying no to tasks that are not critical to achieving your goals. It's easy to get distracted by small details and tactical tasks that are not important. By saying no to these tasks, you can free up more time and resources to strategically focus on the tasks that are critical to achieving your goals.

In conclusion, prioritisation is key to achieving success. By identifying what is most important and focusing on those areas, you can make the most of your time and resources. Use tools like the Eisenhower Matrix and the 80/20 rule to help you prioritise your tasks. Remember to say no to tasks that are not critical to achieving your goals. With a clear focus on what is most important, you can achieve your goals and succeed in your personal and professional life.

10 journaling prompts

1. What are the most important goals you want to achieve in the next six months?

2. What tasks or activities are currently distracting you from achieving your most important goals?

3. How can you prioritise your time and focus on the activities that will contribute the most to achieving your goals?

4. What criteria do you use to determine what is most important in your work or personal life?

5. Are there any tasks or activities that you can delegate or eliminate to free up more time for your top priorities?

6. How do you stay focused and avoid getting sidetracked by minor details or interruptions?

7. What strategies have you found effective for prioritising your work when you have multiple competing demands?

8. How do you balance short-term and long-term priorities in your work and personal life?

9. Are there any tools or techniques you use to help you prioritise your time and stay focused on your goals?

10. What are some strategies for overcoming procrastination and taking action on your most important priorities?

Chapter 8 Being proactive

Anticipate future challenges and opportunities. Think ahead and plan for potential outcomes.

Being proactive is an essential characteristic of successful individuals, businesses, and organisations. Proactivity involves taking control of one's life and future by anticipating future challenges and opportunities and planning for potential outcomes. It is about thinking ahead and taking steps to avoid or mitigate potential problems while maximising potential opportunities. By being proactive, individuals can minimise the risk of failure, achieve their goals, and ensure their future success.

To be proactive, one must first understand the environment they are operating in. They must analyse trends, identify potential opportunities and threats, and anticipate the impact of external factors on their lives, businesses, or organisations. This requires a deep understanding of the industry, market, or field in which they operate and an awareness of the current and emerging trends.

Once the external factors have been analysed, individuals must plan for potential outcomes. This involves developing contingency plans, risk mitigation strategies, and action plans to take advantage of opportunities. The plans should be flexible enough to adapt to changing circumstances while being specific enough to provide guidance on what actions should be taken in different situations.

One of the benefits of being proactive is that it allows individuals to take control of their lives and futures. By anticipating challenges and opportunities, individuals can take the necessary steps to achieve their goals and ensure their future success. This can be particularly important in today's rapidly changing world, where new technologies and business models are disrupting traditional industries and creating new opportunities.

Being proactive can also help individuals to avoid potential problems. For example, businesses that are proactive in identifying and addressing potential risks can minimise the likelihood of costly legal, financial, or repetitional problems.

Finally, being proactive is an essential characteristic for leadership. Leaders who are proactive inspire and motivate their teams, create a culture of innovation and risk-taking, and set the direction for their organisations. By being proactive, leaders can anticipate future challenges and opportunities, develop effective strategies, and take the necessary actions to achieve their goals.

In conclusion, being proactive is an essential characteristic for success in today's rapidly changing world. It involves anticipating future challenges and opportunities, thinking ahead, and planning for potential outcomes. By being proactive, individuals can take control of their lives and futures, minimise the risk of failure, and ensure their future success. Being proactive is particularly important for businesses and organisations, as it allows them to adapt to changing circumstances, identify and mitigate potential risks, and take advantage of emerging opportunities.

10 journaling prompts

1. What are some potential challenges or opportunities that you anticipate in the future?

2. How can you prepare for these potential challenges and opportunities?

3. What are some steps you can take to be more proactive in your daily life?

4. How can you improve your ability to anticipate and plan for future events?

5. What are some tools or resources that can help you become more proactive?

6. How can you incorporate proactive thinking into your work or personal relationships?

7. What are some potential risks of not being proactive, and how can you mitigate those risks?

8. How can you encourage others to adopt a proactive mindset?

9. What are some ways that you can stay motivated to be proactive in the face of challenges or setbacks?

10. How can you measure your progress in becoming more proactive and adjust your approach accordingly?

Chapter 9 Fostering a culture of strategic thinking

Encourage others on your team to think strategically. Create an environment that values long-term planning and goal-setting.

Fostering a culture of strategic thinking within a team or organisation can lead to long-term success and growth. It's not enough for only a few individuals to have this mindset; it needs to be embraced by the entire team. Here are some ways to create a culture of strategic thinking:

1. Lead by example: As a leader, it's essential to model strategic thinking. Demonstrate the importance of planning for the future and setting long-term goals. Encourage team members to ask questions, consider the bigger picture and realise the importance of their role and contribution.

2. Encourage questioning: Foster an environment where team members feel comfortable asking questions, challenging assumptions, and thinking critically. This approach can lead to new perspectives and ideas that may not have been considered otherwise. (Some of the journaling prompts in this book could be useful for teams to process individually and collectively. Reach out for Facilitated Sessions www.Camelleilona.com)

3. Value long-term planning: Prioritising long-term planning over short-term gains can lead to sustainable success. Encourage team members to consider the potential impact of their actions on the organisation's future and create plans accordingly.

4. Set clear goals: Setting clear and measurable goals is essential for strategic thinking. Ensure that everyone on the team understands the goals and has a plan for achieving them. This approach can lead to greater focus and alignment within the team.

5. Celebrate successes: Celebrate when goals are achieved or progress is made towards long-term objectives. This approach can help build momentum and motivate team members to continue working towards the organisation's goals.

6. Provide resources: Ensure that team members have the resources they need to think strategically. This may include training or professional development opportunities, access to industry research or data, or collaboration tools to facilitate idea-sharing and planning.

7. Encourage innovation: Encourage team members to think outside the box and come up with new and innovative ideas.

Foster a culture where failure is viewed as an opportunity to learn and improve, rather than a negative outcome.

8. Foster collaboration: Collaboration can lead to new perspectives and ideas that may not have been considered otherwise. Encourage team members to work together and share ideas to develop more robust and strategic plans.

9. Communicate effectively: Communication is critical for strategic thinking. Ensure that everyone on the team understands the organisation's goals and is aware of progress towards achieving them. This approach can help build alignment and prevent misunderstandings.

10. Recognise and reward strategic thinking: Recognise and reward team members who demonstrate strategic thinking skills. This approach can help build a culture that values strategic thinking and encourages others to adopt this mindset.

In conclusion, fostering a culture of strategic thinking requires a deliberate effort from leaders and team members alike. By encouraging questioning, valuing long-term planning, setting clear goals, and providing resources and support, organisations can create an environment that fosters strategic thinking and leads to long-term success.

10 journaling prompts

1. How can you create a culture of strategic thinking within your team or organisation?

2. Who are the people on your team that are already thinking strategically, and how can you encourage and empower them to continue doing so?

3. What are some ways that you can promote the value of long-term planning to your team members?

4. What are some examples of successful companies that have fostered a culture of strategic thinking, and what can you learn from them?

5. How can you incentivise your team members to prioritise strategic thinking and planning over short-term, tactical work?

6. What are some potential roadblocks to creating a culture of strategic thinking, and how can you overcome them?

7. How can you ensure that all team members have a clear understanding of the long-term goals and vision for the organisation?

8. How can you create opportunities for team members to practice and develop their strategic thinking skills?

9. How can you involve team members in the strategic planning process to ensure that everyone feels invested in the long-term success of the organisation?

10. How can you measure the success of your teams efforts to foster a culture of strategic thinking, and what metrics should you use to evaluate progress?

Chapter 10 Measuring progress

Monitor progress towards your goals and adjust your strategy as needed. Celebrate successes and learn from failures.

To ensure that you are on track and making progress, it is important to measure your progress regularly. This allows you to identify what is working well and what needs to be adjusted, and it helps you stay focused on your goals.

Monitoring progress can be done in various ways, depending on the nature of your goals and strategy. Some methods to measure progress include:

1. Setting milestones and timelines: Break down your long-term goals into smaller, manageable milestones, and assign specific deadlines to each one. This helps you track progress and identify any areas that need more attention.

2. Using metrics and KPIs: Develop key performance indicators (KPIs) that are relevant to your goals and strategy, and regularly track these metrics to gauge progress. This can include anything from revenue growth to website traffic to customer satisfaction.

3. Conducting regular check-ins: Schedule regular meetings or check-ins with your team to review progress and discuss any roadblocks or challenges that may be hindering progress.

4. Seeking feedback: Ask for feedback from customers, partners, and other stakeholders to gauge how well your strategy is working and identify areas for improvement.

Once you have established a system for measuring progress, it is important to use the data you collect to make informed decisions and adjust your strategy as needed.

When you achieve a milestone or reach a goal, take the time to acknowledge and celebrate this success. This helps to build momentum and motivate your team to continue working towards the next milestone.

If progress is slower than expected, or if you are not meeting your KPIs, identify the root cause and develop a plan to address it. This may involve adjusting your strategy, reallocating resources, or seeking additional support.

When things do not go according to plan, take the time to reflect on what went wrong and what can be learned from the experience. This helps to prevent similar mistakes in the future and allows you to course-correct and get back on track.

Measuring progress and making adjustments as needed is an ongoing process, and it requires a commitment to continuous improvement. It is important to be flexible and adaptable, and to approach setbacks as opportunities to learn and grow.

In conclusion, monitoring progress towards your goals is a critical component of strategic thinking. By regularly measuring progress, and learning from failures, you can stay focused on your goals and make informed decisions that will help you achieve success.

10 journaling prompts

1. What specific metrics can you use to measure progress towards your goals?

2. How often should you review and adjust your strategy based on progress made towards your goals?

3. What steps can you take to celebrate successes and acknowledge progress made towards your goals?

4. How can you learn from failures and setbacks in order to adjust your strategy moving forward?

5. What role does accountability play in measuring progress towards your goals?

6. How can you stay motivated when progress towards your goals is slow or setbacks occur?

7. What strategies can you use to effectively communicate progress towards your goals to others on your team?

8. What are the potential consequences of not measuring progress towards your goals regularly?

9. How can you stay focused on the big picture while also monitoring progress towards smaller goals?

10. How can you use feedback from others to improve the way you measure and monitor progress towards your goals?

Bonus Chapter Tomorrow AI is Tactical, so Tomorrow we MUST be Strategic

As AI continues to evolve and take on more tactical roles, our ability to think strategically becomes even more critical.

As I was wrapping up this book I was having a conversation about the rapid evolution of artificial intelligence (AI) and how it's transforming the workplace. As AI increasingly handles tactical tasks, we must pivot our focus to strategic thinking. Here we think about how we can embrace this change and prepare for a future where AI handles the tactical so we can focus on the strategic.

Today, AI is already proficient at handling a plethora of tactical tasks, and its capabilities are expanding. Here are a few examples:

Data Entry: AI systems can efficiently process and input vast amounts of data with higher accuracy and speed than humans.

Scheduling: AI-powered tools can manage calendars,

schedule meetings, and even optimise appointment times based on various constraints.

Basic Customer Service: AI chatbots and virtual assistants are adept at handling routine inquiries, providing instant support, and freeing human agents to tackle more complex issues.

Strategic Activities That AI Cannot Replicate

While AI excels at routine and repetitive tasks, it lacks the ability to engage in activities that require human intuition and creativity. Key strategic activities that remain our domain include:

Complex Decision-Making: Humans can analyse nuanced information, weigh ethical considerations, and make decisions that balance short-term gains with long-term impacts.

Ethical Considerations: Addressing ethical dilemmas and ensuring that business practices align with societal values is inherently human.

Creative Problem-Solving: Innovation and creativity are human strengths that AI cannot replicate. Developing new ideas, products, and solutions relies on human ingenuity.

Emotional Intelligence: Building relationships, understanding team dynamics, and providing empathetic leadership are vital skills that AI cannot imitate.

Transition Timeline

The transition from humans performing tactical tasks to AI taking over these responsibilities is already underway. The timeline varies by sector and company, but the change is imminent across all industries. Organisations must recognise this shift and proactively prepare for it.

As AI takes over tactical roles, employees must find their place and relevance within the organisation. This is where a proactive, entrepreneurial mindset becomes essential.

Employees need to develop new skills and mindsets to thrive in this evolving landscape. This thinking journal is a prime example of tools that help employees plan ahead and ensure their positions remain vital.

Preparing for the Future

To thrive in a future dominated by AI in tactical roles, individuals and organisations need to:

Cultivate a Strategic Mindset: Focus on long-term goals, anticipate future challenges, and develop plans to overcome them.

Exercise Creative Thinking: Engage in activities that stimulate the mind and foster innovation. As AI handles the heavy lifting, we must flex our creative muscles.

Embrace Continuous Learning: Develop and refine skills in creative problem-solving, strategic planning, and leadership. Regularly seek out new knowledge and experiences.

As AI continues to evolve and take on more tactical roles, our ability to think strategically becomes even more critical. By focusing on the activities that AI cannot replicate, we ensure our continued relevance and value in the workplace. Tomorrow's success lies in our ability to adapt, learn, and embrace a strategic mindset today.

10 journaling prompts

1. What are some recent decisions I've made that required deep processing? Is there anything about my decision-making process the could be improved?

2. How do I currently gather and assess information for complex decisions? What tools or methods can I use to enhance this process?

3. Think about a tough decision you made in the past year. What were the key factors that influenced your decision, and what would you do differently now?

4. Reflect on an ethical dilemma you've faced at work. How did you handle it, and what did you learn from the experience?

5. List three problems I'm currently facing at work. Brainstorm multiple creative solutions for each one.

6. Reflect on a recent conflict at work. How did I handle it, and what role did emotional intelligence play in resolving it?

7. How do I anticipate the impact of AI on my industry in the next five years? What steps can I take to prepare for these changes?

8. What are some tasks I currently handle that could be delegated to AI? How will this change my daily workflow?

9. Identify a strategic thinker you admire. What can I learn from their approach to problem-solving and decision-making?

10. How can I leverage my emotional intelligence to build stronger relationships and lead more effectively?

Notes

Chapter 7 Prioritizing

1. referred to as Urgent-Important Matrix, helps you decide on and prioritize tasks by urgency and importance, sorting out less urgent and important tasks which you should either delegate or not do at all. https://www.eisenhower.me/eisenhower-matrix/

About the Author

Camelle ilona
Author | Motivational Speaker | Corporate Journaling Facilitator | Corporate Wellbeing Consultant

Helping companies improve workplace culture, advancing their internal talent through corporate journaling and well-being strategies.

With over 15 years of experience in the fashion industry, Camelle ran the international clergy fashion brand, House of ilona. Her invaluable experience in the fashion business culminated in the publication of her first book, "Finding Divine Flow; seeking, finding and flowing in purpose, an entrepreneurial journey." She has gone on to publish many titles, mainly journals packed with prompts to help people process, think deeply and write.

In 2019, Camelle founded and took on the role of Editor-in-Chief for Ordained Magazine, a platform dedicated to amplifying women's voices in ministry. As a leader, she guided a team of over 100 writers and creatives, fostering an environment of writing, collaboration and empowerment. Building upon this success, Camelle founded Divine Flow Publishing, continues supporting authors on their self-publishing journey, and nurtures emerging talents through Divine Flow Academy.

Booking Camelle ilona

Invite Camelle to your
organisation/team to
facilitate corporate
journaling sessions to
think, process and
flow together.
www.Camelleilona.com

Also by Camelle ilona FRSA

Living in the Flow Planner 2024 and **90 Day Planners** (available on Amazon). These are GREAT for keeping on track with your goals, for quarterly and for ticking off your daily habits.

Checkout the new Podcast **"the Journaling experience"** and accompanying journals.

Tactical Today Strategy Tomorrow is a thinking journal for professional growth.

Mother: Beautiful Warrior is 365 journaling prompts for Mom's navigating motherhood while still being true to themselves.

Finding Divine Flow is the first book I wrote but this **Journaling Workbook** takes you on a personal journey of Finding Your Divine Flow.

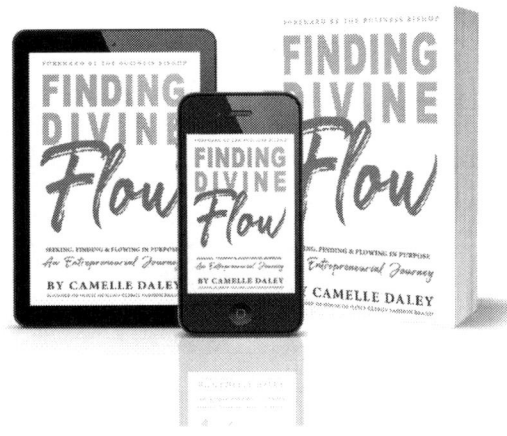

Printed in Great Britain
by Amazon

94c8382c-19b9-4164-a37f-cb796970fcbbR01